I asked God to plant joy
and cheerfulness in your heart.
God made today.
Let's rejoice and be glad.
Very glad.

These things I have spoken to you,
that My joy may remain in you,
and that your joy may be full.
JOHN 15:11 NKJV

Joy is the keynote of the Christian life.
It is not something that happens.
It is a gift, given to us in the coming of Christ.
ELISABETH ELLIOT

I pray
you'll never forget
that each day
is a gift.
That's why they call it
the present.

So teach us to number our days,
that we may present to You
a heart of wisdom.
PSALM 90:12 NASB

*Each day is God's gift
of a fresh, unspoiled opportunity
to live according to His priorities.*
ELIZABETH GEORGE

DaySpring

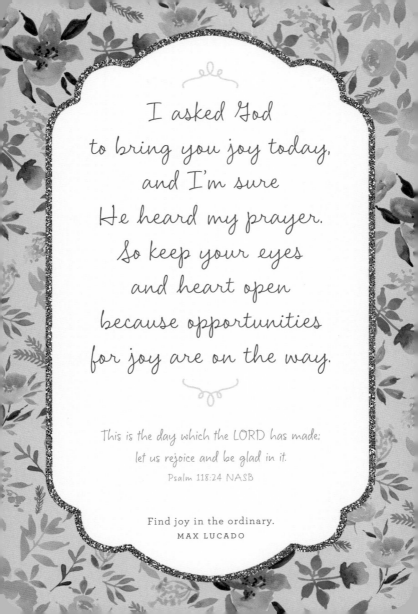

I asked God
to bring you joy today,
and I'm sure
He heard my prayer.
So keep your eyes
and heart open
because opportunities
for joy are on the way.

This is the day which the LORD has made;
let us rejoice and be glad in it.
Psalm 118:24 NASB

Find joy in the ordinary.
MAX LUCADO

DaySpring

I asked God to remind you that
He is your shepherd.
He loves you.
He's watching over you...
and His vision is perfect.

The LORD is my shepherd, I shall not want.
He makes me lie down in green pastures;
He leads me beside quiet waters.
He restores my soul.
PSALM 23:1–3 NASB

Since the Lord is your shepherd,
what are you worried about?
MARIE T. FREEMAN

You're surrounded
by opportunities,
and I asked God
to help you pick the right one.
Or maybe there's more than one.
But don't ask me...ask God.

Thou wilt shew me the path of life:
in thy presence is fulness of joy;
at thy right hand there are
pleasures for evermore.
PSALM 16:11 KJV

God has a course mapped out for
your life, and all the inadequacies
in the world will not change
His mind. He will be with
you every step of the way.
CHARLES STANLEY

DaySpring

I pray that you can visualize
yourself and God together.
Walking together. Working together.
Tackling every challenge together.
Rejoicing together.
Forever.

*But as for you, be strong; don't be
discouraged, for your work has a reward.*
2 CHRONICLES 15:7 HCSB

The power of God through His Spirit will work
within us to the degree that we permit it.
LETTIE COWMAN

God knows that
He did something
very special when
He created you.
I pray that you
know it too.

Finally, brothers, rejoice.
Become mature, be encouraged,
be of the same mind,
be at peace, and the God
of love and peace will be with you.
2 CORINTHIANS 13:11 HCSB

*Resolve never to criticize or downgrade
yourself, but instead rejoice that you
are fearfully and wonderfully made.*
ELIZABETH GEORGE

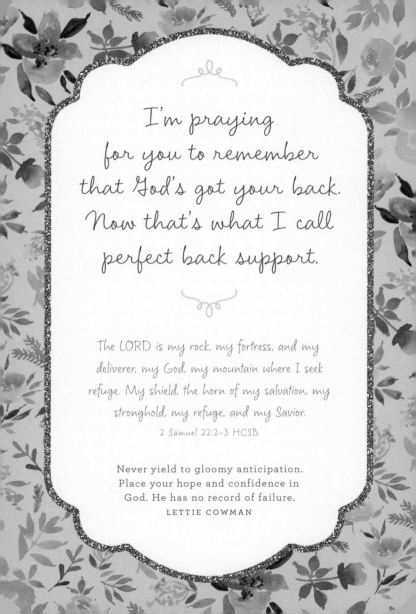

I'm praying
for you to remember
that God's got your back.
Now that's what I call
perfect back support.

The LORD is my rock, my fortress, and my
deliverer, my God, my mountain where I seek
refuge. My shield, the horn of my salvation, my
stronghold, my refuge, and my Savior.
2 Samuel 22:2–3 HCSB

Never yield to gloomy anticipation.
Place your hope and confidence in
God. He has no record of failure.
LETTIE COWMAN

You've got so many possibilities.
I asked God to help you pick
the very best ones. I'm sure
His guidance is on the way.
Soon.

But Jesus looked at them and said
to them, "With men this is impossible,
but with God all things are possible."
MATTHEW 19:26 NKJV

A possibility is a hint from God.
SØREN KIERKEGAARD

When we
run out of gas,
God's still got a full tank.
When we can't do it, He can.
I'm praying you'll depend on Him.
If you've got the faith,
He's got the fuel.

But He said, "The things
which are impossible with men
are possible with God."
LUKE 18:27 NKJV

God is able to do what we can't do.
BILLY GRAHAM

*I said a prayer
for you today, knowing
that God is always
ready to help us.
Our job is to let Him.*

*Therefore humble yourselves under
the mighty hand of God, that He may
exalt you in due time, casting all your
care upon Him, for He cares for you.*
1 PETER 5:6–7 NKJV

God is trying to get a message through to you,
and the message is: "Stop depending on inadequate
human resources. Let me handle the matter."
CATHERINE MARSHALL

You've got friends
who love you and
want to help.
I'm one of them...
but not the only one.

Carry one another's burdens;
in this way you will fulfill
the law of Christ.
GALATIANS 6:2 HCSB

They are rich who have true friends.
THOMAS FULLER

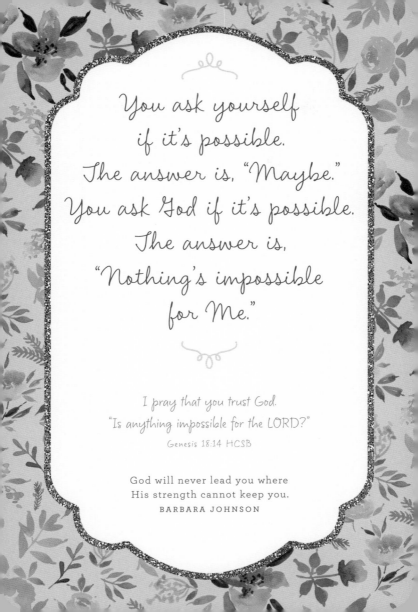

You ask yourself
if it's possible.
The answer is, "Maybe."
You ask God if it's possible.
The answer is,
"Nothing's impossible
for Me."

I pray that you trust God.
"Is anything impossible for the LORD?"
Genesis 18:14 HCSB

God will never lead you where
His strength cannot keep you.
BARBARA JOHNSON

I'm praying
you'll remember that
God loves you...
and so do I.

For the LORD is good. His unfailing love
continues forever, and his faithfulness
continues to each generation.

PSALM 100:5 NLT

We do not need to beg Him to bless us;
He simply cannot help it.

HANNAH WHITALL SMITH

Big Picture:
Everything's Gonna
Be Okay. Little Picture:
Potential Speed Bumps Ahead.
My Prayer: That You'll
Focus on the Big Picture.

Let us hold on to the confession
of our hope without wavering,
for He who promised is faithful.
HEBREWS 10:23 HCSB

God's all-sufficiency is a major.
Your inability is a minor. Major
in majors, not in minors.
CORRIE TEN BOOM

DaySpring

I'm praying that
you'll find joy today.
Lots of it. You and I
both know it's out there.
And I know you can find it.

*Those who listen to instruction will prosper;
those who trust the LORD will be joyful.*
PROVERBS 16:20 NLT

God knows everything. He can manage everything,
and He loves us. Surely this is enough
for a fullness of joy that is beyond words.
HANNAH WHITALL SMITH

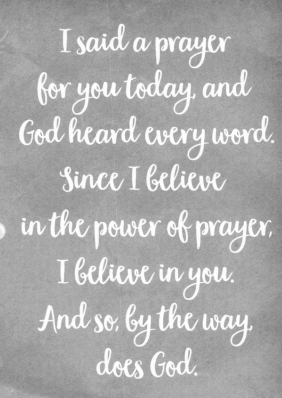

I said a prayer
for you today, and
God heard every word.
Since I believe
in the power of prayer,
I believe in you.
And so, by the way,
does God.

When a believing person
prays, great things happen.
JAMES 5:16 NCV

Prayer is our lifeline to God.
BILLY GRAHAM

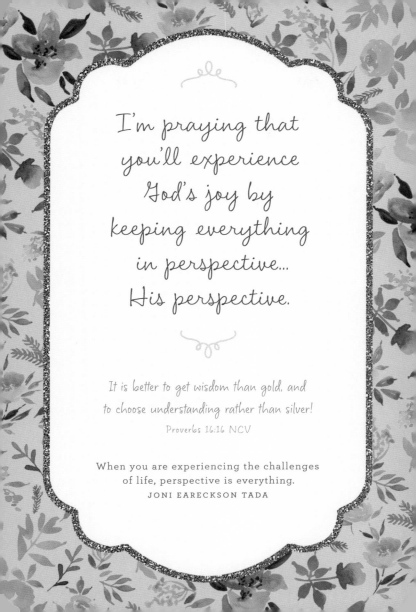

I'm praying that
you'll experience
God's joy by
keeping everything
in perspective...
His perspective.

It is better to get wisdom than gold, and
to choose understanding rather than silver!
Proverbs 16:16 NCV

When you are experiencing the challenges
of life, perspective is everything.
JONI EARECKSON TADA

I'm praying
that you'll take good care...
very good care...
of a very special person:
you.

Come unto me, all ye that labour and
are heavy laden, and I will give you rest.
MATTHEW 11:28 KJV

Life is strenuous.
See that your clock does not run down.
LETTIE COWMAN

Let's rejoice
and pray
without ceasing.
I'm praying for you,
and I hope
you'll keep praying for me.

Rejoice always, pray without ceasing,
in everything give thanks; for this
is the will of God in Christ Jesus for you.
1 THESSALONIANS 5:16–18 NKJV

Any concern that is too small
to be turned into a prayer is
too small to be made into a burden.
CORRIE TEN BOOM

*I'm asking
God to give you
the fullest possible joy...
today, tomorrow,
and forever.
Amen.*

*Until now you have not asked
for anything in my name.
Ask and you will receive,
so that your joy will be
the fullest possible joy.*
JOHN 16:24 NCV

Joy is the serious business of heaven.
C. S. LEWIS

DaySpring

I asked the Lord
to give you strength,
confidence, and joy.
Do you feel it?
I pray that you do.

He gives strength to the
weary, and to him who lacks
might He increases power.
ISAIAH 40:29 NASB

*God meant for life to be filled
with joy and purpose. He invites us
to take our journey with Him.*
BILLY GRAHAM

Congratulations
on a job well done!
I'm praying for your
continued joy and success.
It's wonderful when
nice guys and nice girls
finish first.

Good planning and hard work lead to prosperity...
Proverbs 21:5 NLT

Think of yourself as on the threshold
of unparalleled success. A whole, clear,
glorious life lies before you.
ANDREW CARNEGIE

I asked God
to give you more joy today.
Maybe you already have enough,
but I figured a little
more can't hurt.

Rejoice in the LORD always. Again I will say, rejoice!
PHILIPPIANS 4:4 NKJV

What think we of Christ? Is He altogether glorious
in our eyes and precious to our hearts?
May Christ be our joy, our confidence, our all.
MATTHEW HENRY

I pray you'll
have peace and joy,
knowing that no
challenges are too big for God.
Even big problems are
no problem for Him.

Whatever has been born of God conquers
the world. This is the victory that
has conquered the world: our faith.
1 JOHN 5:4 HCSB

God will make obstacles
serve His purpose.
LETTIE COWMAN

*I pray
(and I believe)
that your hard work
will be rewarded.*

Soon!

*Be strong and courageous, and do the work.
Don't be afraid or discouraged, by the size
of the task, for the LORD God, my God,
is with you. He will not fail
you or forsake you.*
1 CHRONICLES 28:20 NLT

Success actually becomes a habit through the determined
overcoming of obstacles as we meet them one by one.
LAURA INGALLS WILDER

I'm praying
that you remember
we love you.
Always.

❧

Beloved, if God so loved us,
we ought also to love one another.
1 JOHN 4:11 KJV

The best use of life is love.
The best expression of love is time.
The best time to love is now.
RICK WARREN

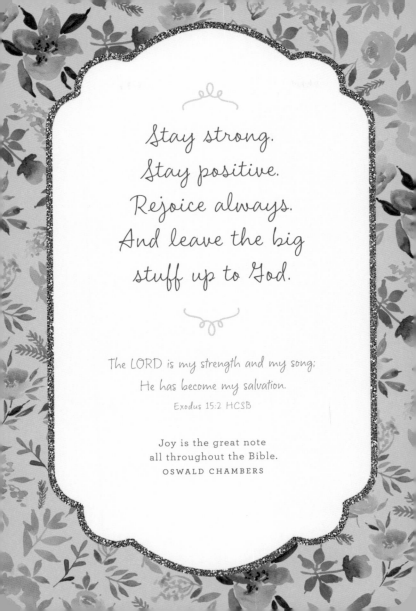

Stay strong.
Stay positive.
Rejoice always.
And leave the big
stuff up to God.

The LORD is my strength and my song;
He has become my salvation.
Exodus 15:2 HCSB

Joy is the great note
all throughout the Bible.
OSWALD CHAMBERS

Today, I told God that
I'm thankful for you.
He knew it already.
And now, so do you.

Enter into His gates with thanksgiving,
and into His courts with praise.
Be thankful to Him, and bless His name.
For the LORD is good; His mercy is everlasting,
and His truth endures to all generations.

PSALM 100:4–5 NKJV

Fill up the spare moments of your life
with praise and thanksgiving.
SARAH YOUNG

I said a prayer
for you today. I asked
the Lord to give you
joy and confidence.
Remember that God is with you
on every step of your journey.
Your dreams are safe with Him.

When doubts filled my mind,
your comfort gave me
renewed hope and cheer.
PSALM 94:19 NLT

Faith expects from God
what is beyond all expectation.
ANDREW MURRAY

I pray that
you'll always ask God
for the things you really need.
He's always listening. And He
wants to hear from you. Now.

Ask, and it will be given to you; seek,
and you will find; knock, and it will be
opened to you. For everyone who asks
receives, and he who seeks finds, and
to him who knocks it will be opened.
MATTHEW 7:7–8 NASB

God will help us become the people we are
meant to be, if only we will ask Him.
HANNAH WHITALL SMITH

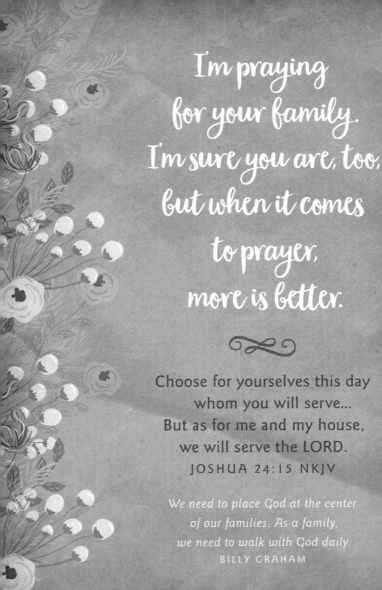

I'm praying
for your family.
I'm sure you are, too,
but when it comes
to prayer,
more is better.

Choose for yourselves this day
whom you will serve...
But as for me and my house,
we will serve the LORD.
JOSHUA 24:15 NKJV

We need to place God at the center
of our families. As a family,
we need to walk with God daily.
BILLY GRAHAM

Today, I pray
that you'll
celebrate your life.
I'm celebrating you,
and God is, too.
Welcome to our
celebration!

Make me hear joy and gladness.
Psalm 51:8 NKJV

There is not one blade of grass,
there is no color in this world, that
is not intended to make us rejoice.
JOHN CALVIN

I pray that you'll keep joy
in your heart today and every day.
God knows that your future
is bright, and I pray that
you'll know it too.

"I say this because I know what
I am planning for you," says the LORD.
"I have good plans for you, not plans to hurt you.
I will give you hope and a good future."
JEREMIAH 29:11 NCV

Our prospects are as bright as the promises of God.
ADONIRAM JUDSON

Optimism pays.
Pessimism costs.
I pray that you'll
stay positive because
the best is yet to come.

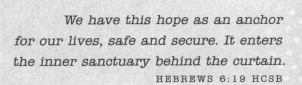

We have this hope as an anchor
for our lives, safe and secure. It enters
the inner sanctuary behind the curtain.
HEBREWS 6:19 HCSB

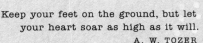

Keep your feet on the ground, but let
your heart soar as high as it will.
A. W. TOZER

I asked God
to bless your next
grand adventure.
I'm praying for you.
I'll help any way I can.
And God will too.

*Do not remember the former things,
nor consider the things of old.
Behold, I will do a new thing.*
ISAIAH 43:18–19 NKJV

God specializes in giving people a fresh start.
RICK WARREN

DaySpring

I pray that you'll remember this: God's got everything under control... so you can relax and rejoice.

God—His way is perfect; the word of the LORD is pure. He is a shield to all who take refuge in Him.
PSALM 18:30 HCSB

God has no problems, only plans.
There is never panic in heaven.
CORRIE TEN BOOM

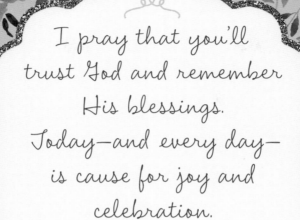

I pray that you'll trust God and remember His blessings. Today—and every day—is cause for joy and celebration.

I will give thanks to the Lord with all my heart;
I will tell of all Your wonders.
I will be glad and exult in You;
I will sing praise to Your name, O Most High.

Psalm 9:1–2 NASB

Two types of voices command your attention today. Negative ones fill your mind with doubt, bitterness, and fear. Positive ones purvey hope and strength. Which one will you choose to heed?

MAX LUCADO

I pray that you'll celebrate
life day by day, one day at a time,
in day-tight compartments.
Every day is a gift and
a cause for celebration.

The LORD reigns; let the earth rejoice.
PSALM 97:1 NKJV

Love, joy, peace, patience, kindness, goodness,
faithfulness, gentleness, and self-control. To these I commit my day.
If I succeed, I will give thanks. If I fail, I will seek His grace.
And then, when this day is done,
I will place my head on my pillow and rest.
MAX LUCADO

I pray you'll
remember that
God is on your side.
And there's no limit
to the things the two
of you can accomplish.

Indeed, *God is my salvation.*
I will trust Him and not be afraid.
ISAIAH 12:2 HCSB

God is the silent partner
in all great enterprises.
ABRAHAM LINCOLN

I'm praying
that you'll do
your best and let God
take care of the rest.

Trust in the LORD with all your heart;
do not depend on your own understanding.
Seek His will in all you do, and
He will show you which path to take.
PROVERBS 3:5-6 NLT

Those who are God's without reserve
are, in every sense, content.
HANNAH WHITALL SMITH

I asked God to remind you that you're getting stronger every day. He knows it, and I know it, and you probably know it too. But it never hurts to be reminded.

Have faith in the LORD your God, and you will stand strong. Have faith in his prophets, and you will succeed.

2 CHRONICLES 20:20 NCV

The strength that we claim from God's Word does not depend on circumstances. Circumstances will be difficult, but our strength will be sufficient.

CORRIE TEN BOOM

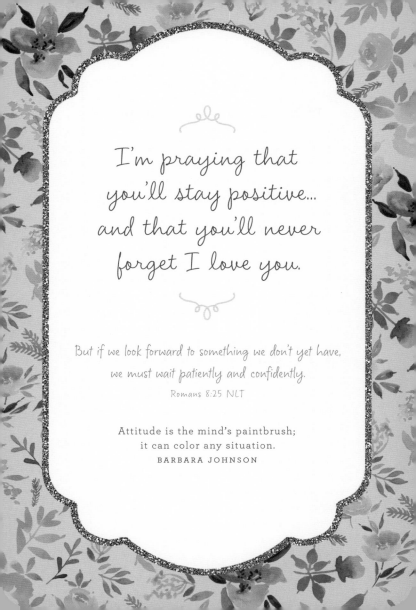

I'm praying that
you'll stay positive...
and that you'll never
forget I love you.

But if we look forward to something we don't yet have,
we must wait patiently and confidently.
Romans 8:25 NLT

Attitude is the mind's paintbrush;
it can color any situation.
BARBARA JOHNSON

I asked God
to remind you that
nothing is impossible for Him.
Zero. Nada.
Absolutely nothing.
Ever.

For with God nothing shall be impossible.
LUKE 1:37 KJV

God is able to do what we can't.
BILLY GRAHAM

I asked God
to remind you that
His timing is perfect.
So don't ever be discouraged.
Your Father has wonderful things
in store for you...now and forever.

For you have need of endurance,
so that when you have done
the will of God, you may
receive what was promised.
HEBREWS 10:36 NASB

How happy we are when we
realize that He is responsible, that
He goes before, that goodness
and mercy shall follow us!
LETTIE COWMAN

Be positive.
Be strong.
Be joyful.
God has everything
under control.

*The LORD is my light and my
salvation—whom should I fear?
The LORD is the stronghold
of my life—of whom should I be afraid?*
PSALM 27:1 HCSB

God will take care of everything—the rest is up to you.
LISA WHELCHEL

I asked God to remind you that it pays to be patient... And I believe your big payday is coming soon.

But if we hope for what we do not yet have, we wait for it patiently.

ROMANS 8:25 NIV

Some of your greatest blessings come with patience.

WARREN WIERSBE

I'm praying that you'll remember this: God's love for you is infinite and eternal. That's a whole lot of love for a very long time. So don't worry; be joyful!

And we have known and believed the love that God has for us. God is love, and he who abides in love abides in God, and God in him.

1 John 4:16 NKJV

God. There is no limit to His power.
There is no limit to His love.
There is no limit to His mercy.
BILLY GRAHAM

Prayer is a worry-extinguisher.
Whenever you're worried
(or whenever you're not),
it's a good time to pray.

Therefore let everyone
who is faithful pray to You...
PSALM 32:6 HCSB

Replace worry with prayer. Make the decision
to pray whenever you catch yourself worrying.
ELIZABETH GEORGE

I asked God
to remind you that
He will never lead you
to a place where His grace
cannot protect you.
The Lord is your shepherd.
Be joyful!

I will lift up my eyes to the hills
from whence comes my help? My
help comes from the LORD, Who
made heaven and earth.
PSALM 121:1-2 NKJV

Trust God's Word and His power more
than you trust your own feelings and
experiences. Remember, your Rock
is Christ, and it is the sea that ebbs
and flows with the tides, not Him.
LETTIE COWMAN

I asked God to give you

joy on your journey,

and I'm sure He heard my

prayer. I pray that more

blessings are on the way. Soon.

*Ask in my name, according to my will,
and He'll most certainly give it to you.
Your joy will be a river overflowing its banks!*
JOHN 16:24 MSG

Our God is so wonderfully good and lovely and
blessed in every way that the mere fact of belonging
to Him is enough for an untellable fullness of joy!
HANNAH WHITALL SMITH

I asked God to remind you that He is always near and that you are always dear to Him. Because God's love never ends, you can rejoice... and I pray that you do.

Shout with joy to the LORD, all the earth! Worship the LORD with gladness. Come before him, singing with joy.
PSALM 100:1–2 NLT

Knowing that your future is absolutely assured can free you to live abundantly today.
SARAH YOUNG

I asked God to remove your concerns and replace them with joy. Has it happened yet?

Now I am coming to You, and I speak these things in the world so that they may have My joy completed in them.
John 17:13 HCSB

Tomorrow is busy worrying about itself; don't get tangled up in its worry-webs.
SARAH YOUNG

Today I asked God to fill
your heart with joy and your mind
with good thoughts. I know
my prayer will be answered
soon. Immediately would be nice.

Finally, brethren, whatever is true, whatever is honorable,
whatever is right, whatever is pure, whatever is lovely,
whatever is of good repute, if there is any excellence
and if anything worthy of praise, dwell on these things.

PHILIPPIANS 4:8 NASB

It is the thoughts and intents of the heart that shape a person's life.

JOHN ELDREDGE

Miracles happen
every day.
Big miracles.
Little miracles.
In-between ones, too.
I'm praying for yours.

*No eye has seen, no ear has heard, no
mind has conceived what God has
prepared for those who love him.*
1 CORINTHIANS 2:9 NIV

Are you looking for a miracle?
If you keep your eyes wide open
and trust in God, you won't
have to look very far.
MARIE T. FREEMAN

*I pray that you'll
celebrate your life today.
And tomorrow.
And every day after day after that.*

Peace I leave with you, My peace
I give to you; not as the world gives
do I give to you. Let not your heart
be troubled, neither let it be afraid.
JOHN 14:27 NKJV

The truth is that even in the midst of trouble,
happy moments swim by us every day,
like shining fish waiting to be caught.
BARBARA JOHNSON

I pray for you to remember that God's got His eye on you. You're safe with Him. Very safe.

But as it is written: What no eye has seen and no ear has heard, and what has never come into a man's heart, is what God has prepared for those who love Him.

1 CORINTHIANS 2:9 HCSB

Before God created the universe, He already had you in mind.
ERWIN LUTZER

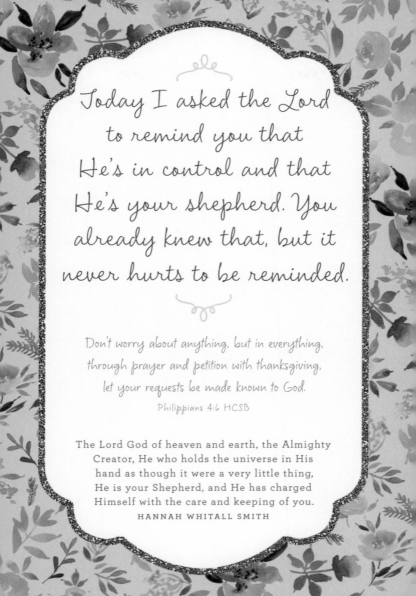

Today I asked the Lord
to remind you that
He's in control and that
He's your shepherd. You
already knew that, but it
never hurts to be reminded.

Don't worry about anything, but in everything,
through prayer and petition with thanksgiving,
let your requests be made known to God.

Philippians 4:6 HCSB

The Lord God of heaven and earth, the Almighty
Creator, He who holds the universe in His
hand as though it were a very little thing,
He is your Shepherd, and He has charged
Himself with the care and keeping of you.

HANNAH WHITALL SMITH

Step by step and day by day, you're going to make it. I asked God to give you patience until you get there.

Better to be patient than powerful;
better to have self-control than to conquer a city.

PROVERBS 16:32 NLT

Faith does not concern itself
with the entire journey. One step is enough.

LETTIE COWMAN

Thanks for
being so kind.
It's people like you
who give friendship
a good name.

Dear friends, let us love one another,
because love is from God,
and everyone who loves has been
born of God and knows God.
1 JOHN 4:7 HCSB

A real friend is one
who helps us to think
our best thoughts,
do our noblest deeds,
and be our finest selves.
ELIZABETH GEORGE

Today, I'm praying
that you'll trust yourself.
And I'm praying
that you'll trust God.
But not necessarily
in that order.

For You are my hope, O LORD God;
You are my trust from my youth.
PSALM 71:5 NKJV

Faith in God is the greatest power,
but great, too, is faith in oneself.
MARY MCLEOD BETHUNE

God is always
with you.
I pray
you'll remember.
that He's not just near.
He's here.

Haven't I commanded you:
be strong and courageous?
Do not be afraid or discouraged,
for the LORD your God is
with you wherever you go.
JOSHUA 1:9 HCSB

Mark it down.
You will never go where God is not.
MAX LUCADO

I thanked God
today for you.
Thanks for all
the nice things you do.
I'm lucky
to be your friend.

No one has ever seen God.
But if we love each other, God lives in us,
and his love is brought to full expression in us.
1 John 4:12 NLT

Friends are like a quilt with lots of
different shapes, sizes, colors, and patterns
of fabric. But the end result brings you
warmth and comfort in a support system
that makes your life richer and fuller.
SUZANNE DALE EZELL

God's peace is always available, 24/7.
His joy is available too.
All day, every day.
So let's celebrate!

A cheerful heart is good medicine,
but a broken spirit saps a person's strength.
PROVERBS 17:22 NLT

Christ can put a spring in your step and a thrill in your heart.
Optimism and cheerfulness are products of knowing Christ.

BILLY GRAHAM

You have
so many talents.
And I'm sure
the world is going to recognize
them sooner or later.
I'm praying for sooner.

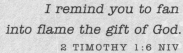

*I remind you to fan
into flame the gift of God.*
2 TIMOTHY 1:6 NIV

You aren't an accident.
You were deliberately planned,
specifically gifted,
and lovingly positioned
on this earth
by the Master Craftsman.
MAX LUCADO

Please keep believing
that God has
big plans for you.
Because He does.

⚜

Anything is possible
if a person believes.
MARK 9:23 NLT

Optimism is that faith that
leads to achievement.
HELEN KELLER

I asked God to help you keep count of your blessings. Of course, there are far too many to count, but it never hurts— and always helps— to try.

Surely the righteous shall give thanks to Your name; the upright shall dwell in Your presence.

PSALM 140:13 NKJV

Receive today's gift gratefully, unwrapping it tenderly and delving into its depths.
SARAH YOUNG

I'm praying that you'll be confident. With your talent—and with God as your Guide and your Protector—your future is so bright, you'd better bring sunscreen.

But if we look forward to something we don't yet have, we must wait patiently and confidently.

Romans 8:25 NLT

The things we think are the things that feed our souls. If we think on pure and lovely things, we shall grow pure and lovely like them; and the converse is equally true.

HANNAH WHITALL SMITH

*I pray you'll
keep thinking good thoughts.
After all, it never hurts
your eyesight to look
on the bright side of things.*

This is the day the LORD has made;
let us rejoice and be glad in it.
PSALM 118:24 HCSB

Life is a glorious opportunity.
BILLY GRAHAM

I prayed
for you today.
I asked God to keep you
in the palm of His hand.
And I asked Him
to bring you joy.
Just thought you'd want to know.

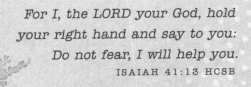

For I, the LORD your God, hold
your right hand and say to you:
Do not fear, I will help you.
ISAIAH 41:13 HCSB

With the goodness of God
to desire our highest welfare,
the wisdom of God to plan it, and
the power of God to achieve it,
what do we lack? The answer, of
course, is that we lack nothing.
A. W. TOZER

*Today, I talked
to God about you.
I asked Him to bless you
and bring you joy. And I believe
He will. Can you feel it yet?*

*The LORD bless you and protect you;
the LORD make His face shine
on you and be gracious to you.*
NUMBERS 6:24–25 HCSB

The power of God through His Spirit
will work within us to the degree that we permit it.
LETTIE COWMAN

I asked God
to give you enthusiasm
for your journey.
If you feel it,
let me know. If not,
I'll keep praying.

Do your work with enthusiasm.
Work as if you were serving
the LORD, not as if you were
serving only men and women.
EPHESIANS 6:7 NCV

Each day, look for a kernel of excitement.
BARBARA JORDAN

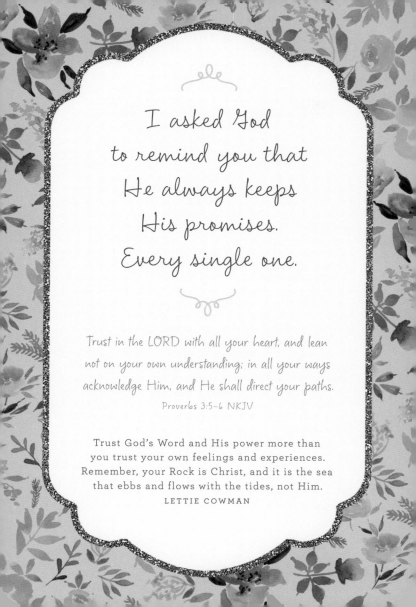

I asked God
to remind you that
He always keeps
His promises.
Every single one.

Trust in the LORD with all your heart, and lean
not on your own understanding; in all your ways
acknowledge Him, and He shall direct your paths.

Proverbs 3:5–6 NKJV

Trust God's Word and His power more than
you trust your own feelings and experiences.
Remember, your Rock is Christ, and it is the sea
that ebbs and flows with the tides, not Him.

LETTIE COWMAN

You've been dreaming
about this fresh start
for a long time.
And now you've begun.
Congratulations!
I'm praying for you.

And my God will supply all your needs
according to His riches in glory in Christ Jesus.
PHILIPPIANS 4:19 HCSB

If you can dream it, you can do it.
WALT DISNEY

I asked the Lord
to remind you that
faith moves mountains.
Then, when I finished praying,
I had a warm, happy feeling
that your mountains
are beginning to move.

For I assure you: If you have faith
the size of a mustard seed, you
will tell this mountain,
"Move from here to there,"
and it will move. Nothing will
be impossible for you.
MATTHEW 17:20 HCSB

Patience and diligence, like
faith, move mountains.
WILLIAM PENN

God loves you so much
that He sent His Son to die for you.
Jesus is the proof of God's love.

For God so loved the world that
He gave His only begotten Son,
that whoever believes in Him should
not perish but have everlasting life.
JOHN 3:16 NKJV

To God be the glory, great things He has done.
So loved He the world that He gave us His Son.
FANNY CROSBY

I asked God to give
you joy today.
I'm certain He
heard my prayer.
So open your heart
to Him, ASAP.

Through the LORD's mercies
we are not consumed,
because His compassions fail
not. They are new every morning;
Great is Your faithfulness.
LAMENTATIONS 3:22–23 NKJV

*All things work together
for good. Fret not, nor fear!*
LETTIE COWMAN

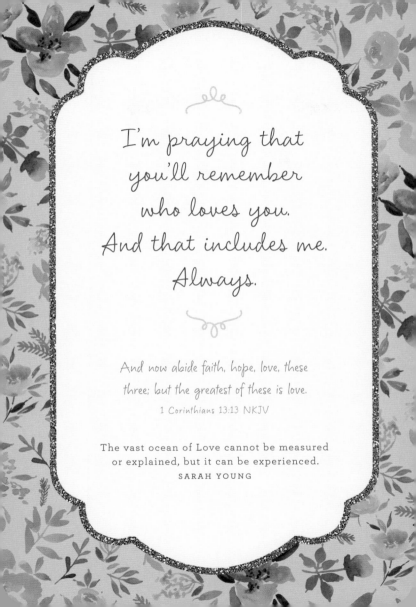

I'm praying that
you'll remember
who loves you.
And that includes me.
Always.

And now abide faith, hope, love, these
three; but the greatest of these is love.
1 Corinthians 13:13 NKJV

The vast ocean of Love cannot be measured
or explained, but it can be experienced.
SARAH YOUNG

If you're ready to make peace with your past, God is ready to help. I pray that when the time is right, you'll talk to Him about it.

The LORD says, "Forget what happened before,
and do not think about the past.
Look at the new thing I am going to do.
It is already happening. Don't you see it?
I will make a road in the desert and
rivers in the dry land."

ISAIAH 43:18–19 NCV

The past cannot be changed, but one's response to it can be.

ERWIN LUTZER

I'm praying that
you'll stay close
to God's Word.
When you let it light
your path, you'll be blessed
today, tomorrow, and forever.

Your word is a lamp to my feet
and a light to my path.
PSALM 119:105 NKJV

Meditating upon His Word will inevitably
bring peace of mind, strength
of purpose, and power for living.
BILL BRIGHT

Today, I prayed that you'll
be joyful and courageous, knowing
that you and God, working
together, can do great things.

The LORD is my light and my salvation—
whom should I fear?
The LORD is the stronghold
of my life—of whom should I be afraid?
PSALM 27:1 HCSB

Faith is not merely holding on to God. It
is God holding on to you.
CORRIE TEN BOOM

You're working hard, and it shows.

I'm praying that you'll finish strong and soon.

Let endurance have its perfect result, so that you may be perfect and complete, lacking in nothing.

JAMES 1:4 NASB

We are all on our way somewhere. We'll get there if we just keep going.

BARBARA JOHNSON

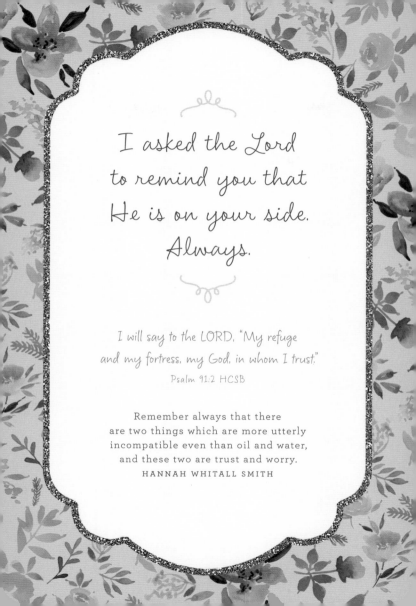

I asked the Lord
to remind you that
He is on your side.
Always.

I will say to the LORD, "My refuge
and my fortress, my God, in whom I trust."
Psalm 91:2 HCSB

Remember always that there
are two things which are more utterly
incompatible even than oil and water,
and these two are trust and worry.
HANNAH WHITALL SMITH

You're on an
important journey.
I'm praying that God
will bring you joy and
peace along the way.

The LORD says, "I will guide you
along the best pathway for your life.
I will advise you and watch over you."
PSALM 32:8 NLT

When we are obedient,
God guides our steps and our stops.
CORRIE TEN BOOM

Today is another
gift from above.
I'm praying that
you'll celebrate God's gift
with joy in your heart
and a smile on your face.

Praise the LORD! Oh, give thanks
to the LORD, for He is good!
For His mercy endures forever.
PSALM 106:1 NKJV

Every day we live is a priceless
gift of God, loaded with possibilities
to learn something new,
to gain fresh insights.
DALE EVANS ROGERS

Today,

*I prayed for you to be strong
and stay strong. There's nothing
you'll face today that you and God,
working together, can't handle.*

*Search for the LORD and for His strength;
continually seek Him. Remember the wonders
He has performed, His miracles,
and the rulings He has given.*
PSALM 105:4–5 NLT

Time spent in prayer will yield more than that
given to work. Prayer alone gives work its worth
and its success. Prayer opens the way for God
Himself to do His work in us and through us.
ANDREW MURRAY

I asked God to shower
you with abundance.
So don't worry if you see
storm clouds overhead.
They're probably just
showers of blessings.

I have come that they may
have life, and that they may
have it more abundantly.

JOHN 10:10 NKJV

God is the giver, and we are the receivers.
And His richest gifts are bestowed not
upon those who do the greatest things,
but upon those who accept
His abundance and His grace.
HANNAH WHITALL SMITH

I pray that you'll keep thinking good thoughts and celebrating your life. It doesn't cost anything to be joyful, and it's a lot more fun than the alternative.

Set your mind on things above,
not on things on the earth.
Colossians 3:2 NKJV

The vigor of our spiritual life will be in exact proportion to the place held by the Bible in our life and thoughts.
GEORGE MÜLLER

Life can be difficult, choices
can be hard, and we all make
mistakes. When you remember
that God has forgiven you,
you can rejoice in His mercy
and His love. I pray that you will.

If we confess our sins, He is faithful and righteous to forgive
us our sins and to cleanse us from all unrighteousness.
1 JOHN 1:9 HCSB

If God forgives us and we do not forgive ourselves,
we make ourselves greater than God.
EDWIN LOUIS COLE

I'm thankful
for you, and
I'm praying for you.
A lot.

Do not worry about anything,
but pray and ask God
for everything you need,
always giving thanks.
PHILIPPIANS 4:6 NCV

God's solution is just
a prayer away!
MAX LUCADO

I asked God
to give you wisdom for your journey.
I know you can make good choices,
but I'm certain that you and
God can make great ones.

*Now if any of you lacks wisdom, he should ask
God, who gives to all generously and without
criticizing, and it will be given to him.*
JAMES 1:5 HCSB

God, give us the grace to accept with serenity
the things that cannot be changed, the courage
to change the things that should be changed,
and the wisdom to distinguish the one from the other.
REINHOLD NIEBUHR

Each new day,
including this one,
is an opportunity to
begin something new.
I'm praying for
your fresh start.

Then He who sat on the
throne said, "Behold,
I make all things new."
REVELATION 21:5 NKJV

There is wonderful freedom
and joy in coming to recognize
that the fun is in the becoming.
GLORIA GAITHER

God has a grand plan for your life. Your life story is being written day by day. I pray—and trust—that your story will be beautiful.

The LORD directs the steps of the godly.
He delights in every detail of their lives.
Though they stumble, they will never fall,
for the LORD holds them by the hand.

Psalm 37:23–24 NLT

Live out your life in its full
meaning; it is God's life.
JOSIAH ROYCE

*I asked the Lord
to give you this message:
With Him on your side,
you have nothing to fear...
and you can do amazing things
through Him. Enough said.*

I can do all things through Christ who strengthens me.
PHILIPPIANS 4:13 NKJV

Do not limit the limitless God! With Him,
face the future unafraid because you are never alone.
LETTIE COWMAN

Today,
I asked God
to give you peace, hope,
courage, and joy. Lots and lots
of peace, hope, courage, and joy.
Know what? I think
He's already answering
my prayer.

And let the peace of God rule
in your hearts, to which
also you were called in one
body; and be thankful.
COLOSSIANS 3:15 NKJV

The most glorious works of grace
that have ever took place,
have been in answer to prayer.
WILLIAM CAREY

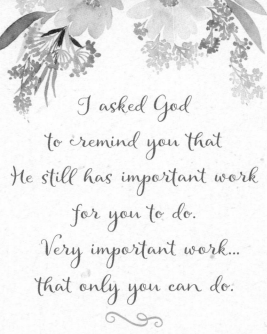

*I asked God
to remind you that
He still has important work
for you to do.
Very important work...
that only you can do.*

*I urge you to live a life worthy
of the calling you have received.*

EPHESIANS 4:1 NIV

Our world is obsessed with success.
But how does God define success?
Success in God's eyes
is faithfulness to His calling.

BILLY GRAHAM

DaySpring

I told God I was
grateful for you.
I'm sure He already
knew it, but I wanted
to tell Him anyway.
And I wanted
to tell you.

Rejoice always,
pray without ceasing,
in everything give thanks;
for this is the will of God
in Christ Jesus for you.
1 THESSALONIANS 5:16–18 NKJV

IT IS ONLY WITH GRATITUDE THAT LIFE
BECOMES RICH. DIETRICH BONHOEFFER

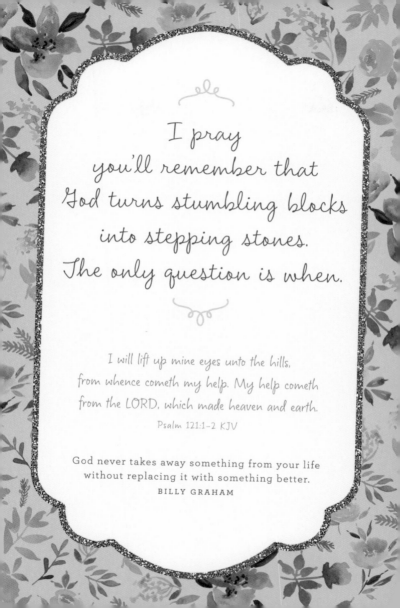

I pray
you'll remember that
God turns stumbling blocks
into stepping stones.
The only question is when.

I will lift up mine eyes unto the hills,
from whence cometh my help. My help cometh
from the LORD, which made heaven and earth.
Psalm 121:1–2 KJV

God never takes away something from your life
without replacing it with something better.
BILLY GRAHAM

God already knows that I'm praying for your speedy recovery. Now you know it too.

Dear friend, I pray that you
may prosper in every way
and be in good health;
physically just as you are spiritually.

3 JOHN 1:2 HCSB

God will keep us. He'll help. He'll intervene—perhaps just
in the nick of time. Is that too close for comfort? Maybe.
But our trust in Him was never meant to be comfortable—
only close. And the nick of time is close enough.

JONI EARECKSON TADA

Today,
I asked God
to remind you how much
you've already accomplished.
You've come a long way, but
the best is yet to come.

Let us hold fast the confession
of our hope without wavering,
for He who promised is faithful.
HEBREWS 10:23 NASB

Remember how far you've come,
not just how far you have to go.
You are not where you want to be,
but neither are you
where you used to be.
RICK WARREN